World's

Greatest

Investors

Jason Mitchell

Jason Mitchell Publishing
1501 Balsam Drive
New Windsor, NY 12553

Ordering Information:
Quantity sales. Special discounts are available on quantity purchases by corporations, associations, and others. For details, contact the publisher at the address above.
Orders by U.S. trade bookstores and wholesalers. Please contact Big Distribution: jakm86@gmail.com

Printed in the United States of America

First Edition

14 13 12 11 10 / 10 9 8 7 6 5 4 3 2 1

Table of Contents

13.   Julian Robertson

14.   Michael Steinhardt

15.   Ralph Wagner

16.   Thomas Rowe Price, Jr.

17.   Bill Miller

18.   Jesse L. Livermore

19.   Philip Fisher

20.   John Bogle

Introduction

So, why a book on these investment titans?

Why not a book on these investment titans! I've been a huge believer that there is not reason to reinvent the wheel.

IT MAKES NO SENSE!!!

I proud myself on finding the masters who've paved the roads for people like me so that I can get to where they were faster, and surpass them to serve my clients needs.

This is why I decided to write this book. Not everyone can afford the 3% management fee, and 30% management fee, but they still want to learn how to invest and trade.

So for those who can't hire a professional or who want to do the work themselves I have written this book for all of you.

You of course will find Warren Buffet, George Soros, Bill Gross, and Peter Lynch here.

But you will also find Jack Bogle, Bill Miller, Michael Steinhardt, and John Templeton.

For this edition we give a brief (sometimes very brief) summary of their lives.

Than we get into the investment philosophy they use, and any books written by them or about them.

Now of course time has come to show that there are many more than just these men, but I believe these investors laid the foundation and paved the path for how so many of us beat the market year after year.

If it wasn't for the men on this list what would the investing landscape look like.

I know that you will find information that will help your investing and trading goals, and give you enough of a foundation to go out and make more money and to continue your study.

David Dreman

Background Information

David Dreman was born in Winnipeg, Canada in 1939. A respected investor, the investment company, Dreman Value Management, where he is the founder and the Chairman, focuses on the assets of pensions, HNW (High Net Worth Individuals), endowments, foundations, and mutual funds.

His father, Joseph Dreman, was a prominent trader on the Winnipeg Commodity exchange for many years. I guess you can say that David had his choice of career chosen for him from the very start.

David Dreman, went to school at the University of Manitoba (graduated in 1958).

After graduating Dreman went to work as Director of Research for Rauscher Pierce; senior investment officer with Seligman; and senior editor of Value Line Investment Services.

Dreman founded his first investment firm, Dreman Value Management, Inc., and serves as its president chairman.

Dreman has published many scholarly articles and written four books.

He has is a contributor to Forbes Magazine as a writer, and is on the Board of Directors of the Institute of Behavioral Finance.

Dreman is most famous for his contrarian value investing strategies. Strategies that Warren Buffet is also very famous for…you can see why this is one strategy I enjoy employing.

Investment Philosophy

How did Dreman come to his contrarian investment style?

Well its said that he, like so many other greats, learned his lesson from a painful experience.

The story goes that in the year 1969, while working as a junior analyst, he followed the crowd and bought shares of a company that skyrocketed based off speculation. The earnings of the company were non-existent.

He is quoted as saying, "I invested in the stocks du jour and lost 75% of my net worth."

Following his huge mistake of being a sheep and following the herd, he became obsessed with how psychology affects investors and the market as a whole.

Thus the birth of his contrarian value investing style.

When interviewed for Kiplinger Personal Finance Magazine in 2001 he explained his approach as buying out of favor battered stocks. Very strict in his discipline, he said he always buys stocks with low P/E ratios, low Price-to-Book Value Ratios, and higher than average yield.

Academic studies and real life examples have shown that buying out-of-favor stocks with low P/E, Price to Book, and Price to Cash ratios outperform the market consistently over the long term.

David Dreman Books

- Contrarian Investment Strategy: The Psychology of Stock Market Success
- Contrarian Investment Strategies: The Next Generation
- Psychology and the Stock Market: Investment Strategy Beyond Random Walk
- The New Contrarian Investment Strategy
- Contrarian Investment Strategies: The Psychological Edge

David Dreman Scholarly Articles (Sample of the vast amount)

- Investor Overreaction: Evidence that its Basis is Psychological
- A Report on the March 2001 Investor Sentiment Survey
- Bubbles and the Role of Analysts' Forecasts
- Do Contrarian Strategies Work Within Industries?
- Analyst Forecast Errors and Their Implications for Security Analysis

William H. Gross

Background Information

William (Bill) Hunt Gross (born April 13th, 1944, in Middletown, Ohio), to Shirley Tait, a homemaker, and Sewell Mark Gross, a sales executive for AK Steel Holding.

Originally, from Winnipeg, Canada he relocated to San Francisco with his family in 1954.

Graduating from Duke University in 1966 with a degree in psychology; served in the Navy, earning his MBA from UCLA Anderson School of Management in 1971.

Gross had a brief stint as a professional blackjack player in Vegas. He is known for saying that

As an American Money Manager and an author, he co-founded Pacific Investment Management Co. (PIMCO), and runs PIMCO's $270 billion Total Fund Return (PTTRX).

Gross manages one of the world's largest mutual funds, focusing mostly on funds.

The New York Times calls Gross "the nation's most prominent bond investor".

Investment Philosophy

Bill Gross believes that successful investing, doesn't matter if it is in equities or bonds, rest on two foundations:

1.   Having a long term view of the market
2.   Having a strategy for your portfolio and the composition of the portfolio

Gross' explanation of these foundations is having a 3-5 year forecast of the market. The reason for this is to keep focused on the big picture and not sway by the daily fluctuations in the market.

Gross is concerned that if you have a short term view point you will succumb to the emotional ups and downs of fear and greed.

Gross is clear in saying that, "such emotions can convince any investor or management firm to do exactly the wrong thing during irrational periods in the market."

William Gross is quoted as saying, "those who fail to recognize the structural elements of the investment equation will leave far more chips on the table for other more astute investors to scoop up than they could ever imagine."

What are those structural elements of the investment equation that Gross is talking about...they are:

- Asset allocation
- Diversification
- Risk-return measurements

- Investing cost

Publications

- Bill Gross On Investing
- Bond King: Investment Secrets From PIMCOs Bill Gross
- Everything You've Heard About Investing Is Wrong: How To Profit In The Coming Post-Bull Markets

Peter Lynch

Background Information

Peter Lynch (born in Newton, Massachusetts, in 1944) graduated from Boston College in 1965 with a degree in finance.

After Boston College, Lynch went to serve two years in the military before graduating from Wharton School at the University of Pennsylvania with a MBA in 1968.

With his degree in hand, Lynch went to work for Fidelity Investments as an investment analyst. He eventually became the firm's director of research, a position he held from 1974 to 1977.

Lynch was named manager of the little known Magellan Fund in 1977 and achieved historic portfolio results in the ensuing years until his retirement in 1990.

At the time of his taking over the Magellan Fund in 1977, it had only $18 million in assets. By the time he resigned in 1990, the fund had grown to over $14 billion in assets.

The fund did an impressive average annual return of 29.2%.

In 2007, Peter Lynch was serving as vice-chairman of Fidelity's investment adviser, Fidelity Management & Research Co. Since his retirement, he has been an active participant in a variety of philanthropic endeavors.

Lynch now operates as a research consultant for Fidelity.

Investment Philosophy

Peter Lynch had what would now be referred to as a flexible fund or a multi-strategy fun (Hedge Fund World).

Meaning that he was a chameleon, adapting to whatever style best worked at the time. He is known for having a work schedule that was the perfect example of a 24/7 lifestyle.

He talked to industry experts, investment professionals, company executives, and analyst around the clock.

With such a grueling work schedule, Peter Lynch had to have a very strict discipline and set of guidelines and principles to his stock selection process.

Lynch checklist is:

1. Know what you own
2. It's futile to predict the economy and interest rates
3. You have plenty of time to identify and recognize exceptional companies
4. Avoid long shots
5. Good management is very important – buy good businesses
6. Be flexible and humble, and learn from mistakes.

7.   Before you make a purchase, you should be able to explain why you're buying

8.   There's always something to worry about.

When it came to picking stocks, Lynch stuck to businesses that he knew or could easily understand. This was very important to him.

He also had a very strong belief in research and doing due diligence when getting into an investment. Lynch as a bottom-up investment type of investor was focused on a company's fundamentals.

Peter Lynch was not interested in short-term market fluctuations…he was only interested in investing for the long term.

Publications

- Learn To Earn
- One Up On Wall Street
- Beating The Street

William J. O'Neil

Background Information

William J. O'Neil (born in Oklahoma City, Oklahoma; March 25th, 1933) is a writer, stockbroker, and American entrepreneur, who founded the business newspaper Investor's Business Daily and founded the stock brokerage firm William O'Neil & Co. Inc.

O'Neil studied business at Southern Methodist University, receiving a Bachelor's degree and serving in the US Air Force.

After the Air Force, he started his career as a stockbroker with Hayden, Stone, & Company in 1958. He developed his CANSLIM investment strategy at that firm...making him the highest performing broker in his firm.

His professional and financial successes gave him the ability to form his own brokerage firm, the William O'Neil & Co. Inc.

O'Neil became the youngest member at 30 years old (at the time), to buy a seat on the New York Stock Exchange.

Investment Philosophy

O'Neil has a performance based investment style that blends qualitative and quantitative strategies. His investment style is to find growth stocks that have the greatest chance to have a huge price rise from the moment they are purchased.

Bill O'Neil's motto is "buy the strong, sell the weak."

His criteria for identifying a stock that can head to new heights are in his investment strategy CANSLIM.

C - Current quarterly earnings per share have increased sharply from the
same quarters' earnings reported in the prior year (at least 25%).

A - Annual earnings increases at a compound rate of no less than 25%
(P/E is unimportant – probably in the range of 20-45 with these stocks) annual over the last five years.

N - New management, new products, and new highs. Stocks that have a
good story.

S - Supply and demand. The less stock that is outstanding the more
buying demand will drive the prices higher. Look for stocks that have 10 to 20 million shares outstanding.

L - Leaders and laggards. Stick with Best of Breed only. Find those stocks
that outperform and leave the rest behind.

I - Institutional Ownership. Choose companies that don't have a lot of
shares owned by top professional investors. This is for many reasons...one being that if they have to sell they can drop the price significantly for any and all reasons.

M - Market direction. Buy stocks that are on a major downturn, but make
sure, you are buying a solid company with a broken stock...not the other way around.

Publications

- The Successful Investor
- How To Make Money In Stocks
- 24 Essential Lessons For Investment Success

James D. Slater

Background Information

James D. Slater was born in the UK in 1929.

Starting as an accountant and then going into management for a number of manufacturing firms, between 1953 and 1963.

With his business partner, Peter Walker, founded the investment company Slater Walker Securities, in 1964.

Using his firm, Slater became a major player in the UK business world, becoming famous for hostile takeovers. Using this aggressive corporate takeover strategy, Slater built the firm into a Financial and Industrial Conglomerate...later becoming an Investment Bank.

1973-74 left Slater filing for personal bankruptcy due to a severe UK recession, ending his firm Slater Walker Securities.

He fought his way back to solvency through private investing and through the launch of a career as a financial writer.

His widely read investment column, "The Capitalist," and extremely popular investment advisory service called "Company REFS," which provided "really essential financial statistics" on all publicly traded U.K. companies, positioned Slater as an investment savant.

He became known as one of his country's most successful professional investors. A parallel career as an educator of individual investors.

In 2007, he remained active today as a major investor in a variety of small, growth-oriented companies.

Investment Philosophy

Slater's favorite type of investment was small cap growth stocks.

He liked to get into them before they became known by the rest of the investment community and really took off.

Slater was the inventor of the PEG ratio. This is the tool he used to determine his investment decisions. This equation combines both growth and value investing…comparing a companies price to earnings multiple with their estimated growth rate.

Slater realized that a P/E ratio didn't mean that a stock was expensive as long as its earnings growth was high.

For example, if company's stock was at a relatively high P/E of 30, but its earnings were expected to grow at a rate of 30%, it would have a PEG of 1, which is generally considered a very favorable value relationship.

Slater pioneered the use of the PEG ratio, which today is widely used in investment analysis.

Publications

- How To Become A Millionaire
- Make Money While You Sleep
- Investments Made Easy
- The Zulu Principle: Making Extraordinary Profits from Ordinary Shares
- Beyond The Zulu Principle: Extraordinary Profits From Growth Shares

John Templeton

Background Information

John Marks Templeton (born November 29th, 912; Winchester, TN) was an investor and mutual fund pioneer. He attended Yale University, graduating in 1934 near the top of his class.

He attended Oxford University as a Rhodes Scholar and earned an M.A. in law.

More of a spiritualist and nor favoring the dogma of religion, Templeton lived an open and honest approach believing that all faiths had something to teach us.

He was a lifelong member of the Presbyterian Church.

He served as an elder of the First Presbyterian Church of Englewood (NJ). He was a trustee on the board of Princeton Theological Seminary, the largest Presbyterian seminary, for 42 years and served as its chair for 12 years.

Templeton became a billionaire by pioneering the use of globally diversified mutual funds.

His Templeton Growth Fund, Ltd., established in 1954, was among the first who invested in Japan in the middle of the 1960s.

One of the biggest things he is known for is, during the Depression of the 1930s, buying 100 shares of each stock listed on the NYSE which was then selling for less than $1 a share.

He bought shares in over 104 companies, in 1939, later making many times the money back when USA industry picked up because of World War II.

In 2006, he was listed in a seven-way tie for 129th place on the *Sunday Times* "Rich List". He rejected technical analysis for stock trading, preferring instead to use fundamental analysis.

Money magazine in 1999 called him "arguably the greatest global stock picker of the century"

Templeton was one of the most generous philanthropists in history, giving away over $1 billion to charitable causes.

Templeton renounced his U.S. citizenship in 1964, thus allowing him to channel an additional $100 million that he would have paid in U.S. income taxes when he sold his international investment fund, toward philanthropy.

He had dual naturalized Bahamian and British citizenship and lived in the Bahamas, where he died at the age of 95 in 2008.

Investment Philosophy

Templeton is known as one of the past century's top contrarians.

One quote about Templeton is, "he bought low during the Depression, sold high during the internet boom and made more than a few good calls in between."

His investing style can be as he called it "bargain hunting, "by searching out such targets in many countries instead of just one that are value investments.

Templeton's investing mantra was "search for companies around the world that offered low prices and an excellent long-term outlook."

As a value-contrarian investor, Templeton believed that the best bargains were in stocks that were completely neglected - those that other investors were not even studying.

In this regard, he had an advantage not readily available to the average individual investor – his residence in Lyford Cay in the Bahamas. The Lyford Key Club was populated with successful businessmen from all parts of the world.

Templeton found he could easily exchange ideas and opinions with them in that attractive ambiance, which, for him, worked better than networking with Wall Street contacts with limited information who were always trying to sell him things.

Not unlike fellow legendary investor Phillip Fisher, Templeton systematically mined his numerous contacts for valuable, objective investment data, which in his case related to market conditions and investment targets around the world.

Publications:

- Golden Nuggets from Sir John Templeton
- Worldwide Laws of Life: 200 Eternal Spiritual Principles

- Investing the Templeton Way: The Market Beating Strategies of Value Investing Legendary Bargain Hunter
- Riches for the Mind and Spirit: John Marks Templeton's Treasury of Words to Help, Inspire, and Live By
- Spiritual Investments: Wall Street Wisdom From The Career Of Sir John Templeton
- Buying at the Point of Maximum Pessimism: Six Value Investing Trends from China to Oil to Agriculture

Warren Buffet

Background Information

Where some of the great investors written in this book will be familiar and others will not be, you have to be living under a rock to not know about Warren Buffet (born August 30th, 1930; Omaha, Nebraska).

Warren Buffett graduated from the University of Nebraska in 1950 with a Bachelor of Science degree.
Being a man of action he went to Columbia University, after reading "The Intelligent Investor" (by Benjamin Graham), because he wanted to study under Graham.

Buffet obtained his Master of Science degree in business in 1951.

After his stint in NYC, Buffet returned to Omaha and formed the investment firm Buffett-Falk & Company, and worked as an investment salesman from 1951 to 1954.

During this time, Buffett developed a close relationship with Graham, who was generous with his time and thoughts.

This interaction between the former professor and student eventually landed Buffett a job with Graham's New York firm, Graham-Newman Corporation, where he worked as a security analyst from 1954 to 1956.

Those two years of working side-by-side with Graham, analyzing hundreds of companies were very instructive and formative years that formed the foundation for Buffett's approach to successful stock investing.

Wanting to work independently, Buffett returned home once again to Omaha and started a family investment partnership at age 25 with a starting capital base of $100,000.

From 1956 to 1969, investors, including Buffett, experienced a thirty-fold gain in their value per share.

Before deciding to end the investment partnership (because the market was very inflated and overvalued), the final decision to liquidate the partnership, Buffett had acquired the unprofitable Berkshire Hathaway textile company in New Bedford, Massachusetts.

After acquiring Berkshire, Buffett successfully turned around the company…that focused on changing the company's financial framework.

Buffet used Berkshire as a holding company for other investments.

During the stock market crash of 1973-74, Buffet was on a buying spree, and started positions in some of his most famous stocks such as the Washington Post. Berkshire Hathaway is now a mammoth holding company with annual sales in the hundreds of billions of dollars range.

Investment Philosophy

Warren is quintessential contrarian-value investor. He is a investor of patience, value, and discipline and has outperformed the market consistently for decades.

Buffet believes in buying great companies that you should feel comfortable owning for years.

He is not ashamed to say that when you go into a business, you should think that this is the only business you will ever own, and if it still makes sense after thinking it is the only business you will ever own than you should buy it. Only at a price that makes business sense of course.

Buffet looks for companies that have great management that can run and grow the business; strong earnings; low to no debt; profits in the form of cash flow; and he has to understand the business and how it makes money.

Buffet is so patient that he will keep a company on his shopping list for years...making sure the fundamentals are improving while he waits for the market to give it to him at a great buying price.

Publications

Warren is one of the few investment luminaries to not have penned a book or two, but his annual reports are famous for his investment criteria, style, and insights. You can find them on the company's main website.

Carl Icahn

Carl Icahn was born in February 16, 1936, in Far Rockaway, Queens NYC into a middle-class family.

Thanks to a scholarship, he managed to attend and graduate from Princeton University with a degree in Philosophy. He later attended New York University's School of Medicine, but dropped out before he graduated.

The story goes that he didn't like corpses so he needed a change of focus.

He took an entry-level stockbroker job with Dreyfus & Company in NYC. 1968, he bought a seat on the NYSE and his finance career really started with him trading mostly options.

Icahn started to develop what we now call an activist investing strategy. Buying controlling interest in public companies forcing them to make changes that increase the value of the company, and the stock for himself and the other shareholders.

Icahn started his corporate raiding activities in earnest in the late 1970s and hit the big leagues with his hostile takeover of TWA in 1985.

Known as an extremely tough negotiator and a clever strategist, whose persistence and personality quirks often distracted his opponents...a string of corporate battles included such names as RJR Nabisco, Texaco, Phillips Petroleum, Western Union, Gulf & Western, Viacom, Revlon, Kerr-McGee, Time Warner and Motorola.

Because of his substantial fortune, Icahn has become a major philanthropist, especially with donations to his alma mater, Princeton University.

Accordingly, he has been the recipient of a number of civic awards for his work and contributions to public health, medical research and education charities in the New York area.

Investment Philosophy

Fortune Magazine in a May 2007 article states, "the most competitive person I know ... he's especially good at terrorizing people and wearing down their defenses." For most people, especially the corporate executives who've dealt with Icahn can attest that this is his investment strategy and business operandi.

Icahn's strategy involves targeting a company he thinks is poorly run and whose stock price is trading below value.

He thrives when the markets are on a downtrend; when everyone else is selling, he starts buying. He accumulates enough of an ownership position to lobby for a position on the company's board of directors.

Usually his first demand is to dump the CEO and, oftentimes, to consider breaking up the company into separate parts and selling them off.

Wall Street professionals say that most of the time he is successful because he's intimidating and relentless.

He's viewed as such a surefire moneymaker that investment managers typically start buying up the company's stock, which, whether Icahn is successful or not, leaves him with healthy stock price gains.

A classic example of this phenomenon is Icahn's push in 2006 to oust CEO Richard Parsons and break up Time Warner. It didn't work out that way.

When Icahn was asked about his failed attempt in a February 2007 *Time Magazine* interview, Icahn said "… Dick Parsons agreed to do what we wanted most - a $20 billion buyback of the stock. He did what he promised, and the stock is up 30%. That helps shareholders. Our [hedge] fund made $250 million. It's a nice way to lose."

So how has Icahn's investment style worked out?

A 2007 *Fortune Magazine* profile reported "in its less-than-three-year existence, the Icahn Partners hedge fund has posted annualized gains of 40%; after fees, investors pocketed 28%.

That 40% gain trounces the S&P 500's return of around 13%, as well as the 12% for all hedge funds calculated by the HedgeFund.net research firm."

Publications

Icahn like Buffet hasn't put pen to paper as an author. But there is a book written about his life.

- King Icahn

John Neff

Background Information

John Neff (born 1931 in Wauseon, Ohio) is one of the best-known mutual fund investors of the last 40 years. He is notable for his contrarian and value investing styles as well as heading Vanguard's Windsor Fund.

During Neff's tenure, Windsor became the best performing mutual fund and thus the largest…making news for closing its doors to new investors in the 1980s.

Neff retired from Vanguard in 1995…and during his 31 years at the helm, Windsor returned 13.7% against the S&P doing 10.6% during the same time.

Investment Philosophy

John Neff did not describe himself as either a value or a contrarian investor.

He preferred instead to characterize his investing approach to one of buying "good companies, in good industries, at low price-to-earnings prices."

Despite his value-contrarian investor disclaimer, Neff's investment management career shows a considerable amount of this type of investing strategy.

Neff practiced portfolio concentration over diversification.

He pursued stocks of all sizes – large, small, and medium – as long as they evidenced low P/E ratios, which he described as "low P/E investing."

Two of Neff's favorite investing tactics, were to (1) buy on bad news after a stock had taken a substantial plunge and (2) to take "indirect paths" to buying in to popular industries.

This involved, for example, buying manufacturers of drilling pipe that sold to the "hot stock" (too pricey for Neff) oil service companies.

He preached against participating in "adrenaline markets" (momentum driven) and preferred face-to-face meetings with a company's management to assess its integrity and effectiveness.

For most individual investors, this type of contact is not a realistic possibility; however, using Neff's rigorous fundamental analysis techniques as applied to a company's financials will turn up enough management performance indicators to compensate for the inability to directly interact with a company's managers.

As noted by Ryan Furman in his July 2006 interview with Neff for the Motley Fool, "most great investors are serious bookworms."

John Neff is no exception: "He gained notoriety for taking all of his weekly *Wall Street Journal* copies home for a second read during the weekend." Furman also reported that Neff reads *Value Line* religiously.

Neff preferred to dig into the company via non-tech ways…such as interviewing the management, and digging into the financials. He wasn't a statistical investor.

Like Warren Buffet, Neff put great emphasis on the ROE. By measuring the return on equity, you can tell a management's true ability to grow and manage a business.

Publications

- John Neff on Investing

George Soros

Background Information

George Soros was born in Budapest, Hungary in August 12, 1930. His birth name was Schwartz György.

Due to social-politic climate in Hungary Soros fled to England where graduated from London School of Economics...leading him to taking a entry-level job at an investment bank in London.

In 1956, he immigrated to the United States and held analyst and investment management positions at the New York firms of F.M. Mayer (1956-59), Wertheim & Co. (1959-63) and Arnhold & S. Bleichroeder (1963-73).

Soros went off on his own in 1973, founding the hedge fund company of Soros Fund Management, which eventually evolved into the well-known and respected Quantum Fund.

For almost two decades, he ran this aggressive and successful hedge fund, reportedly racking up returns in excess of 30% per year and, on two occasions, posting annual returns of more than 100%.

Soros gave up the day-to-day management of the Quantum Fund during the late 1980s. As one of the wealthiest people in the world, Soros became a substantial philanthropist, donating huge sums worldwide through his Open Society Foundation.

In recent years, political activism has also become important to Soros.

He has written and lectured extensively on the role of the U.S. in world affairs as well as issues dealing with, among others, human rights, political freedom and education.

Investment Philosophy

George Soros was a master at translating broad-brush economic trends into highly leveraged, killer plays in bonds and currencies.

Soros was a short-term speculator, making huge bets on the directions of financial markets.

He believed that financial markets can best be described as chaotic.

The prices of securities and currencies depend on human beings, or the traders - both professional and non-professional - who buy and sell these assets. These persons often act out based on emotion, rather than logical considerations.

He also believed that market participants influenced one another and moved in herds.

He said that most of the time he moved with the herd, but always watched for an opportunity to get out in front and "make a killing."

How could he tell when the time was right?

Soros has said that he would have an instinctive physical reaction about when to buy and sell, making his strategy a difficult model to emulate.

When he fully retired in 2000, he had spent almost 20 years speculating with billions of other people's money, making him - and them - very wealthy through his highly successful Quantum Fund.

He made some mistakes along the way, but his net results made him one of the world's wealthiest investors in history.

Publications

- The Bubble Of American Supremacy: Correcting The Misuse Of American Power
- Soros On Soros: Staying Ahead Of The Curve
- The Alchemy Of Finance
- Open Society: Reforming Global Capitalism
- Soros: The Life And Times Of A Messianic Billionaire

Benjamin Graham

Background Information

Benjamin Graham (b. May 8th, 1894 – d. September 21st, 1976) was a British born American investor and author.

Graham is considered the father of value investing…something he started teaching when he was at Columbia Business School and refined with his business partner David Dodd, through various editions of Security Analysis.

Graham had many disciples in his lifetime the most famous being Warren Buffet, Irving Kahn, Walter J. Schloss, and William J. Ruane.

His partnership with Jerome Newman in 1926 gave birth to the firm Graham-Newman Partnership. When he retired in 1956, the firm had a healthy average annual return of 17%.

Investment Philosophy

Morningstar's online Interactive Classroom carries this anecdote about the results of Ben Graham's investing style:

"In 1984, (Warren) Buffet returned to Columbia to give a speech commemorating the fiftieth anniversary of the publication of "Security Analysis". During that speech, he presented his own investment record as well as those of Ruane, Knapp, and Schloss (other successful investment managers who were students of Graham at Columbia). In short, each of these men posted investment results that blew away the returns of the overall market. Buffett noted that each of the portfolios varied greatly in the number and type of stocks, but what did not vary was the managers' adherence to Graham's investment principles."

It is hard to capture what Graham stood for in a few paragraphs much less a few sentences. I urge you to go and purchase a copy of the Intelligent Investor to get a full understanding of his investing approach.

The essence of Graham's value investing is that any investment should be worth substantially more than an investor has to pay for it.

He believed in thorough analysis, which we now call fundamental analysis. He sought out companies with strong balance sheets, or those with little debt, above-average profit margins, and ample cash flow.

He coined the phrase "margin of safety" to explain his common-sense formula that seeks out undervalued companies whose stock prices are temporarily down, but whose fundamentals, for the long run, are sound.

The margin of safety on any investment is the difference between its purchase price and its intrinsic value or net worth.

The larger this difference is (purchase price below intrinsic), the more attractive the investment - from both a safety, and return perspective - becomes.

The investment community commonly refers to these circumstances as low value multiple stocks.

Graham also believed that market valuations (stock prices) are often wrong.

He used his famous "Mr. Market" parable to highlight a truth: stock prices will fluctuate substantially in value.

His philosophy was that this feature of the market offers smart investors "an opportunity to buy wisely when prices fall sharply and to sell wisely when they advance a great deal."

Publications

- The Intelligent Investor
- Security Analysis
- Benjamin Graham: The Memoirs Of The Dean Of Wall Street

Julian Robertson

Background Information

Robertson (born June 25th, 1932; North Carolina) now a retired hedge fund manager, invest mostly in getting other hedge funds started by his former employees at the now defunct Tiger Management.

Robertson graduated from the University of North Carolina with a degree in business administration in 1955.

After time in the Navy, he joined Kidder, Peabody & Co. in New York in 1957 and, over a twenty-year career, became one of the firm's top producing stockbrokers, becoming head of Kidder Peabody's money management subsidiary, Webster Management Corporation.

He started on his own investment/hedge fund firm, Tiger Management Group, in 1980.
One of the earliest hedge funds.

The firm enjoyed year after year of brilliant returns turned a reported $8 million investment in 1980 into $7.2 billion in 1996. During the later part of this period, Robertson was the reigning titan of the world's hedge funds.

At his peak, no one could best him for sheer stock-picking acumen. Investors, at a required minimum initial investment of $5 million, flocked into his six hedge funds.

In the late 1990s, Robertson was upset over the tech-stock craze and, avoided what he considered "irrational" investing. The TMG funds missed out on any participation on the big gains of the sector...despite the overvalued stocks their was quick money to be made.

The gradual demise of Tiger from 1998 to 2000, when all its funds were closed, was reflected in the plunge in assets under management from a high of $23 billion to a closing value of $6 billion.

Poor stock picking and large, misplaced bets on risky market trades are cited as the cause of Robertson's downfall.

However, it is felt by many objective observers that high-level executive defections from TMG's management, as well as Robertson's autocratic managerial style and notorious temper, eventually took their toll on the firm's performance.

While continuing to manage his own investments, Robertson retired from the hedge fund business. He is active in philanthropy and supporting the resolution of environmental issues.

His 2003 estimated net worth was over $400 million, and in March 2011, it was estimated by *Forbes* at $2.3 billion.

Robertson said in 2008 that he shorted subprime securities and made money through credit default swaps. The following year, according to *Forbes*, Robertson's return on his $200 million personal trading account was 150 percent.

Investment Philosophy

Honestly there isn't much to be said about Robertson's investment style. There is very little the average investor can use with regard to Robertson's approach to investing.

It was highly personal.

In TMG, Robertson would get input from his analysts and make all the investment decisions.

There are stories that say Robertson was a macro trader, and often rode worldwide trends. He argued against using fundamentals, a position that well might have led to the poor performance and liquidation of his Tiger funds in 2000.

His investment style, about which there is very little written, consisted of a "smart idea, grounded on exhaustive research, followed by a big bet."

Not exactly a practical framework that would work for the general investing public.

Robertson's highly individualized approach served him well for a time, but when the end came, it was abrupt - not a unfamiliar phenomenon in the world of hedge fund investing.

Publications

Robertson never wrote any books himself, but one was written about him.

- Julian Robertson: A Tiger in the Land Of Bulls And Bears

Michael Steinhardt

Background Information

Michael H. Steinhardt (born December 7th, 1940 in Brooklyn, NY) is known as an American Hedge Fund manager, investor, financier, philanthropist active in Jewish causes, and a newspaper publisher.

A graduate of Wharton School of Business at the University of Pennsylvania, and founded his hedge fund Steinhardt, Fine, Berkowitz & Co., in 1967

Under Steinhardt's direction, the firm consistently found successful macro market moves and then fit securities trading strategies into these situations.

In 1979, Berkowitz and Fine left the partnership, which was then renamed as Steinhardt Partners.

Steinhardt's spectacular career ended in 1995 when he decided to close the business with his fortune and reputation intact after his fund gained 21% in its last year.

This was a year removed from the tough loss that he suffered in 1994, when interest rates moved against him, which produced a 30% loss for his fund...

Steinhardt ended his career on an upswing.

Steinhardt turned to philanthropic activities and served on the boards of many institutions such as New York University, University of Pennsylvania, and Wisdom Tree Investments.

Investment Philosophy

Steinhardt had a long-term investor's perspective but, for the most part, invested as a short-term strategic trader.

He bet on directional moves using an eclectic mix of securities and was backed up by a team of traders and analysts.

He emphasized macro asset allocation type moves from which he harvested his gains.

Charles Kirk, publisher of *The Kirk Report*, gleaned these "rules of investing" from a Steinhardt speech back in June, 2004, which shows that even a high-flying hedge fund investor needs to be grounded:

- Make all your mistakes early in life. The more tough lessons early on, the fewer errors you make later.
- Always make your living doing something you enjoy.
- Be intellectually competitive. The key to research is to assimilate as much data as possible in order to be to the first to sense a major change.

- Make good decisions even with incomplete information. You will never have all the information you need. What matters is what you do with the information you have.
- Always trust your intuition, which resembles a hidden supercomputer in the mind. It can help you do the right thing at the right time if you give it a chance.
- Don't make small investments. If you're going to put money at risk, make sure the reward is high enough to justify the time and effort you put into the investment decision.

Publications

- No Bull: My Life In And Out Of Markets

Ralph Wanger

Background Information

Ralph Wanger (born in Chicago in 1933) received both his bachelors and masters from MIT (Massachusetts Institute of Technology), in 1955.

Starting as an insurance salesman, Wanger began investing with Harris Associates in Chicago.

There he worked as a securities analyst and portfolio manager until the formation of the Acorn Fund in 1977…at which time he became its portfolio manager and president.

He held this position until his retirement in 2003.

While the S&P 500 Index climbed 12.1% per year during this period, Acorn racked up an annualized 16.3% return.

Investment Philosophy

Wanger's investing style at Acorn was simple:

1. Be a long-term holder of smaller companies with financial strength,
2. Look for entrepreneurial managers and
3. Look for understandable businesses that will benefit from a macroeconomic trend.

He's quoted as saying, "If you're looking for a home run – a great investment for five years or ten years or more – then the only way to beat this enormous fog that covers the future is to identify a long-term trend that will give a particular business some sort of edge."

Wanger employed the idea of investing according to "themes."

For example, if he had been around during the California gold rush, he would not have been investing in gold claims, but he would have loved the businesses that sold miners their picks and shovels.

The mines played out in a matter of months, but gold diggers kept at it for several years.

It is reported that Wanger was a voracious consumer of investment information. In valuing a company to invest in, he looked for the following parameters:

- A growing market for the company's product or service
- Evidence of a company's dominant market share
- Outstanding management
- An understandable business
- Evidence of a company's marketing skills
- A high level of customer service
- Opportunity for a large stake in the company
- A strong balance sheet

- The price must be attractive

Lastly, Wanger said he constantly had to remind himself that you can have a good company but a bad stock.

Publications

- Zebra In Lion Country

Thomas Rowe Price, Jr.

Background Information

Thomas Rowe Price, Jr. (born 1898 in Linwood, Maryland; died 1983) was the founder of T. Rowe Price an American publicly owned investment firm.

A graduate of Swarthmore College with a degree in Chemistry.

Price first entered the world of Wall Street investing in the 1920s.

By 1937, he founded his investment firm, T. Rowe Price, in Baltimore, Maryland.

Between 1937 and 1971, when he sold his firm to his employees, Price gradually developed a theory that investing was superior to speculating.

Price is best known for developing the growth stock style of investing, for which he has been called "the father of growth investing".

Price believed that investors could earn superior returns by investing in well-managed companies in fertile fields whose earnings and dividends could be expected to grow faster than inflation and the overall economy.

The core of Price's approach, proprietary research to guide investment selection and diversification to reduce risk, has remained part of the firm's principles.

Investment Philosophy

Thomas Rowe Price's investment management philosophy was based on investment discipline, process consistency and fundamental analysis.

He created the methodology of growth investing by focusing on well-managed companies in "fertile" fields whose earnings and dividends were expected to grow faster than inflation and the overall economy.

John Train, author of "The Money Masters", says that Price looked for these characteristics in growth companies:

- Superior research to develop products and markets.
- A lack of cutthroat competition.
- A comparative immunity from government regulation.
- Low total labor costs, but well-paid employees.
- At least a 10% return on invested capital, sustained high profit margins, and a superior growth of earnings per share.

Price and his firm became extremely successful employing the growth stock approach to buying stocks.

By 1965, he had spent almost thirty years as a growth advocate. At that time, many of his favorite stocks became known in the market as "T. Rowe Price stocks."

However, by the late '60s, he had become wary of the market's unquestioning enthusiasm for growth stocks – he felt the time had come for investors to change their orientation.

He thought price multiples had become unreasonable and decided that the long bull market was over. This is when he began to sell his interests in T. Rowe Price Associates.

By 1973-1974, what Price's forecast took shape and growth stocks fell hard and fast.

Much to Price's dismay, his namesake firm barely managed to survive. Obviously, the term, "irrational exuberance" didn't exist in those days, but its destructive force was well appreciated by Thomas Rowe Price.

Publications

Never wrote any books on his investment style or anything else.

There are books with Price mentioned like: The Money Masters.

Bill Miller

Background Information

Bill Miller is the former CEO and Chairman of Legg Capital Management, a subsidiary of Legg Mason, Inc. (born in Laurinburg, North Carolina, in 1950).

Miller is formerly the portfolio manager of the Legg Mason Capital Management Value Trust, and is currently the portfolio manager of the Legg Mason Opportunity Trust mutual funds, run by Miller through Legg Mason subsidiary LMM.

Miller is also Chairman Emeritus of the Santa Fe Institute.

A graduate from Washington and Lee University in 1972 with a degree in Economics.

Investment Philosophy

Fortune Magazine's managing editor, Andy Serwer, characterized Bill Miller's investing style as iconoclastic: "You simply can't do what he's done in the supremely competitive, ultra-efficient world of stock picking by following the pack ... The fact is that Miller has spent decades studying freethinking overachievers, and along the way he's become one himself."

Bill Miller is a self-described value investor, but his definition of value investing is disturbing to some traditional value investors.

Miller believes that any stock can be a value stock if it trades at a discount to its intrinsic value.

Individual investors can learn from Miller's application of this investing principle, which, he says, was the basis for the 15-year benchmark-beating record of the Legg Mason Value Trust fund.

He attributes two factors to this success:
- exhaustive security analysis and
- portfolio construction.

In his 2006, fourth-quarter letter to the shareholders for Value Trust, Bill Miller explains how these two factors work:

Value investing means really asking what are the best values, and not assuming that because something looks expensive that it is, or assuming that because a stock is down in price and trades at low multiples that it is a bargain ... Sometimes growth is cheap and value expensive. . . . The question is not growth or value, but where is the best value ... We construct portfolios by using 'factor diversification.' . . . We own a mix of companies whose fundamental valuation factors differ. We have high P/E and low P/E, high price-to-book and low-price-to-book.

Most investors tend to be relatively undiversified with respect to these valuation factors, with traditional value investors clustered in low valuations, and growth investors in high valuations ... It was in the mid-1990s that we began to create portfolios that had greater factor diversification, which became our strength ...We own low PE and we own high PE, but we own them for the same reason: we think they are mispriced.

We differ from many value investors in being willing to analyze stocks that look expensive to see if they really are. Most, in fact, are, but some are not. To the extent we get that right, we will benefit shareholders and clients.

Publications

- The Man Who Beats The S&P: Investing With Bill Miller

Jesse L. Livermore

Background Information

Jesse Lauriston Livermore (July 26, 1877 – November 28, 1940; Shrewsbury, Massachusetts) was an American stock trader.

He was most famous for making and losing several multi-million dollar fortunes and short selling during the stock market crashes in 1907 and 1929.

He then began trading for himself and by the age of fifteen.

Over the next several years, he made money betting against the so-called "bucket shops," which didn't handle legitimate trades – customers bet against the house on stock price movements.

He did so well that he was banned from all of the shops in Boston, which prompted his move, at age 20, to New York.

In New York is where his speculative trading successes - and failures - made him a celebrity on Wall Street and around the world. His financial difficulties finally ended tragically with his suicide death at the age of 63.

Investment Philosophy

Jesse Livermore had no formal education or stock trading experience.
He was a self-made man who learned from his winners as well as his losers.

It was these successes and failures that helped cement trading ideas that can still be found throughout the market today.

Some of the major principles that he employed include:

- Money is not made in day trading on price fluctuations. Livermore emphasized the importance of focusing on markets as a whole, rather than on individual stocks. He noted that greater success comes from determining the direction of the overall market than attempting to pick the direction of an individual stock without concern for market direction.
- Adopt a buy-and-hold strategy in a bull market and sell when it loses momentum. Livermore always had an exit strategy in place.
- Study the fundamentals of a company, the market and the economy. Livermore separated successful investors from unsuccessful investors by the level of effort they put into investing.
- Investors who focus on the short term eventually lose their capital.
- Ignore insider information; make your own independent analysis. Livermore was very careful about where he got his information and recommended using multiple sources
- Embrace change in adapting investing strategies to evolving market conditions

Publications

- How to Trade in Stocks
- Jesse Livermore – Speculator King
- Trade Like Jesse Livermore
- Reminiscences of a Stock Operator

Philip Fisher

Background Information

Philip Arthur Fisher (September 8, 1907 – March 11, 2004; San Francisco, California) was an American stock investor best known as the author of *Common Stocks and Uncommon Profits*, a guide to investing that has remained in print ever since it was first published in 1958.

Philip Fisher's career began in 1928 when he dropped out of the newly created Stanford Business School to work as a securities analyst with the Anglo-London Bank in San Francisco.

He switched to a stock exchange firm for a short time before starting his own money management business as Fisher & Company in 1931. He managed the company's affairs until his retirement in 1999 at the age of 91, and is reported to have made his clients extraordinary investment gains.

Although he began some fifty years before the name Silicon

Valley became known, he specialized in innovative companies driven by research and development.

He practiced long-term investing, and strove to buy great companies at reasonable prices.

He was a very private person, giving few interviews, and was very selective about the clients he took on.

He was not well known to the public until he published his first book in 1958.

Philip Fisher was one of the most influential investors of all time. His investment philosophies, recorded in his investment classic, "Common Stocks and Uncommon Profits" (1958) are still relevant today and are widely studied and applied by investment professionals.

It was the first investment book ever to make the *New York Times* bestseller list. Fisher\'s son, Kenneth L. Fisher, wrote a eulogy for his father in his regular column in *Forbes* magazine (March 11, 2004):

"Among the pioneer, formative thinkers in the growth stock school of investing, he may have been the last professional witnessing the 1929 crash to go on to become a big name. His career spanned 74 years, but was more diverse than growth stock picking. He did early venture capital and private equity, advised chief executives, wrote and taught. He had an impact. For decades, big names in investing claimed Dad as a mentor, role model and inspiration."

Investment Philosophy

Fisher achieved an excellent record during his 70 plus years of money management by investing in well-managed, high-quality growth companies, which he held for the long term.

For example, he bought Motorola stock in 1955 and didn't sell it until his death in 2004.

His famous "fifteen points to look for in a common stock" were divided up between two categories:

1.   management's qualities and
2.   the characteristics of the business.

Important qualities for management included integrity, conservative accounting, accessibility and good long-term outlook, openness to change, excellent financial controls, and good personnel policies.

Important business characteristics would include a growth orientation, high profit margins, and high return on capital, a commitment to research and development, superior sales organization, leading industry position and proprietary products or services.

Philip Fisher searched everywhere for information on a company.

A seemingly simplistic tool, what he called "scuttlebutt," or the "business grapevine," was his technique of choice.

He devotes a considerable amount of commentary to this topic in "Common Stocks And Uncommon Profits". He was superb at networking and used all the contacts he could muster to gather information and perspective on a company. He considered this method of researching a company to be extremely valuable.

Publications

- Common Stocks And Uncommon Profits
- Developing An Investment Philosophy
- Conservative Investors Sleep Well

John Bogle

Background Information

John Bogle (born May 8th, 1929; Montclair, New Jersey) is the founder and retired CEO of The Vanguard Group. He is known for his 1999 book *Common Sense on Mutual Funds: New Imperatives for the Intelligent Investor*, which became a bestseller and is considered a classic.

Bogle went to Princeton University to get his undergraduate degree...leading him to next attend the University of Pennsylvania, taking night and weekend classes.

He learned the investment management business by working for financial advisor Wellington Management from 1951 to 1974 and founded Vanguard in 1974.

As president of Vanguard's Bogle Financial Markets Research Center, he continues to write and lecture on investment issues and is widely recognized as "the conscience" of the mutual fund industry.

Investment Philosophy

Jack Bogle's investing philosophy advocates capturing market returns by investing in broad-based index mutual funds that are characterized as no-load, low-cost, low-turnover and passively managed.

Bogle is consistent in his insistence, especially in various media appearances and in writing, on the superiority of index funds over traditional actively managed mutual funds.

He insists that it is stupid to attempt to pick actively managed mutual funds and expect their performance to beat a low-cost index fund over a long period of time...especially after accounting for the fees that actively managed funds charge.

Bogle argues for an approach to investing defined by simplicity and common sense.

Here are some of his key points to remember and follow:

- Do not overrate past fund performance
- Don't own too many funds
- Buy your fund portfolio – and hold it
- Beware of asset size
- Beware in Mutual Fund Star Managers
- Consider the added cost of advice
- Select Cost Advice
- Rely on rational analysis and an avoidance of emotions in investment-decisions

Publications

- Common Sense On Mutual Funds: New Imperatives For The Intelligent Investor
- John Bogle On Investing: The First 50 Years
- Bogle On Mutual Funds
- The Little Book Of Common Sense Investing: The Only Way To Guarantee Your Fair Share Of Stock Market Returns
- The Vanguard Experiment: John Bogle's Quest To Transform The Mutual Fund Industry

About Jason Mitchell

Jason Mitchell is the stimulating, truth-telling modern Renaissance Man; a serial, successful entrepreneur; trusted marketing advisor, singer, consultant and coach to hundreds of private entrepreneurial clients running businesses from $5-million to $10-billion in size.

As a speaker, Jason delivers content that enriches, inspires, changes, and challenges all those in attendance.

An expert on topics such as investing, real estate, personal development, relationships, sex, life, spirituality, and self improvement Jason is never without something to say and share that leaves his audience feeling like they have earned more than their money's worth.

As a singer, Jason is asked to perform in a number of genres and styles. From gospel to rock, jazz to blues, opera to musicals, R&B to Pop Jason leaves the crowd wanting more, and always gives his absolute best. Jason takes on corporate gigs, music festivals, and other venues commanding top fees from those who want a professional.

When you call Jason you get a rich deep bass-baritone voice that leaves you remembering his name and feeling like part of the family. Mostly doing private parties and events getting paid upward of $50,000 to $75,000 Jason only takes on gigs where he can add value, leave a lasting impression, and where he feels he can give his clients the best.

As a direct-response marketing consultant and copywriter, Jason is the "secret sauce" behind full-page magazine ads, TV infomercials, online marketing and direct mail. He is routinely paid upwards from $50,000.00 to, on average, $100,000.00 to $200,000.00 plus royalties to craft direct-response ads, sales letters, direct-mail campaigns and integrated offline/online marketing systems for his private clients…

He has created winning campaigns for health, diet and beauty products and companies, B2B and industry products including software, and the finance and investment markets — Jason does a massive amount of work in the information-marketing industry including book, home study course, online course and newsletter publishers; seminar, conference and event promoters; coaching organizations; and associations. Most new client relationships begin with an initial consulting day at his base fee of $20,000.00, conducted in one of his homes, or $40,000 if you want him to come to you. There is usually a waiting list, and new client candidates are asked to communicate initially via a one to two page memo describing their business, needs and interests.

To see about hiring Jason for work as a consultant for your business, to manage your portfolio, or anything else e-mail jakm86@gmail.com and your request will be processed and you will be alerted as to the next step.